LEARN TO DRAW

Disney · PIXAR

TOY STORY

Featuring favorite characters from Toy Story 2 & Toy Story 3!

Illustrated by the Disney Storybook Artists

The library edition published in 2011 by Walter Foster Publishing, Inc.
Walter Foster Library
Distributed by Black Rabbit Books.
P.O. Box 3263 Mankato, Minnesota 56002

Printed in Mankato, Minnesota, USA by CG Book Printers, a division of Corporate Graphics.

First Library Edition

Library of Congress Cataloging-in-Publication Data

Learn to draw Disney/Pixar Toy Story: featuring favorite characters from Toy Story 2 & Toy Story 3! / illustrated by the Disney Storybook Artists. -- 1st library ed.
    p. cm.
 ISBN 978-1-936309-00-9 (hardcover)
 1. Cartoon characters--Juvenile literature. 2. Drawing--Technique--Juvenile literature. 3. Toy story (Motion picture)--Juvenile literature. 4. Toy story 2 (Motion picture)--Juvenile literature. 5. Toy story 3 (Motion picture)--Juvenile literature. I. Disney Publishing Creative Development (Firm) II. Pixar (Firm) III. Disney Storybook Artists. IV. Walter Foster (Firm)
 NC1764.L34 2010
 741.5'1--dc22
                                                                                              2010003775

012011
17254

9 8 7 6 5 4 3 2

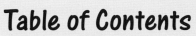

Table of Contents

Disney · PIXAR
TOY STORY

As *Toy Story* begins, the toys in Andy's room are nervous. Andy, the young boy who plays with them, is about to have a birthday party. Birthday parties mean presents . . . and presents mean new toys. Rex (the toy T. Rex), Slinky Dog, Mr. Potato Head, Hamm (the piggy bank), and the others worry that new toys will take their place. Woody, the cowboy doll who has been Andy's favorite toy for years, tells them not to worry. The most important thing, he reminds them, is that they are all there for Andy.

Woody has to follow his own advice when he sees Andy's newest toy. It is a Buzz Lightyear action figure, with karate-chop motions, laser lights, and pop-out wings. Strangely, Buzz does not realize he is a toy. He believes he is a genuine space ranger, sworn to protect the universe from the evil Emperor Zurg.

Woody tries to keep Buzz from becoming Andy's top toy. But his plan lands both of them in the hands of Sid, the toy-destroying boy next door. Woody and Buzz have to work with each other—and with some very scary mutant toys—to make their way back to Andy. Along the way, they become friends and realize that they are both important to Andy.

Disney · PIXAR
TOY STORY 2

In *Toy Story 2*, when Woody tries to help save an older toy from a yard sale, he ends up toy-napped! Al, of Al's Toy Barn, nabs Woody in order to complete his collectible set of toys from *Woody's Roundup,* an old black-and-white TV show.

Al plans to sell the set to a toy museum in Japan. In Al's apartment, Woody meets the rest of his Roundup gang: Bullseye, the sharpest horse in the West; Jessie, the yodeling cowgirl; and the Prospector, the mint-condition miner.

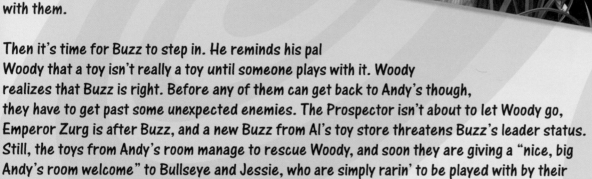

Meanwhile, Buzz and the others from Andy's room race to rescue their pal. After a long adventure, the toys finally arrive at Al's place, where they learn that Woody now *likes* being a collectible! He doesn't want to go back to Andy's room. It turns out the other collectible toys in Al's apartment have convinced him he'll end up in the next yard sale if he doesn't choose to stay with them.

Then it's time for Buzz to step in. He reminds his pal Woody that a toy isn't really a toy until someone plays with it. Woody realizes that Buzz is right. Before any of them can get back to Andy's though, they have to get past some unexpected enemies. The Prospector isn't about to let Woody go, Emperor Zurg is after Buzz, and a new Buzz from Al's toy store threatens Buzz's leader status. Still, the toys from Andy's room manage to rescue Woody, and soon they are giving a "nice, big Andy's room welcome" to Bullseye and Jessie, who are simply rarin' to be played with by their new kid, Andy.

TOOLS AND MATERIALS

crayons

colored pencils

eraser

paintbrush

ink pen

Here are some tools you might need while drawing your favorite *Toy Story* characters: a drawing pencil, an eraser, colored pencils, a pencil sharpener, crayons, felt-tip markers, paint and paintbrushes, and an ink pen. Be sure to have plenty of paper on hand for practice!

drawing pencil

paint palette

pencil sharpener

GETTING STARTED

Just follow these simple steps, and you'll be amazed at how fun and easy drawing can be!

STEP 1 Draw the basic shape of the character; then add simple guidelines to help you place the features.

STEP 2 Each new step is shown in blue. Simply follow the blue lines to add the details.

STEP 3 Erase any lines you don't want to keep.

STEP 4 Use crayons, markers, colored pencils, or paints to add color.

SPACE RANGER   LIGHTYEAR

WOODY

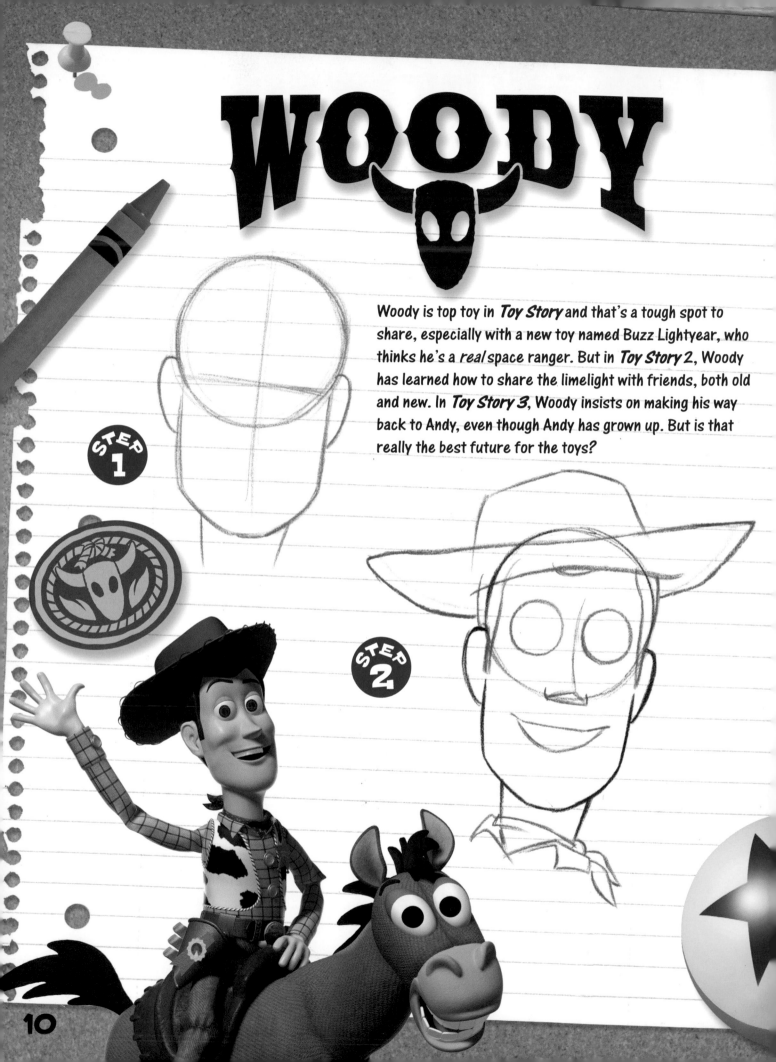

STEP 1

STEP 2

Woody is top toy in *Toy Story* and that's a tough spot to share, especially with a new toy named Buzz Lightyear, who thinks he's a *real* space ranger. But in *Toy Story 2*, Woody has learned how to share the limelight with friends, both old and new. In *Toy Story 3*, Woody insists on making his way back to Andy, even though Andy has grown up. But is that really the best future for the toys?

round eyes

large iris

STEP 3

ears are flat on top

YES!

NO! too straight

YES! teeth are one long rectangle

NO!

Buzz lightyear

Buzz has stars in his eyes until Woody pulls him back down to earth. For most of *Toy Story*, Buzz doesn't understand that he's a toy. But in *Toy Story 2*, he understands so well that he has to remind Woody. In *Toy Story 3*, Buzz is captured by a gang of hostile toys, who switch his setting to "demo." Woody and the others rescue him, but when they try to restore his setting, they accidentally switch his language button to Spanish!

STEP 1

STEP 2

angled

straight

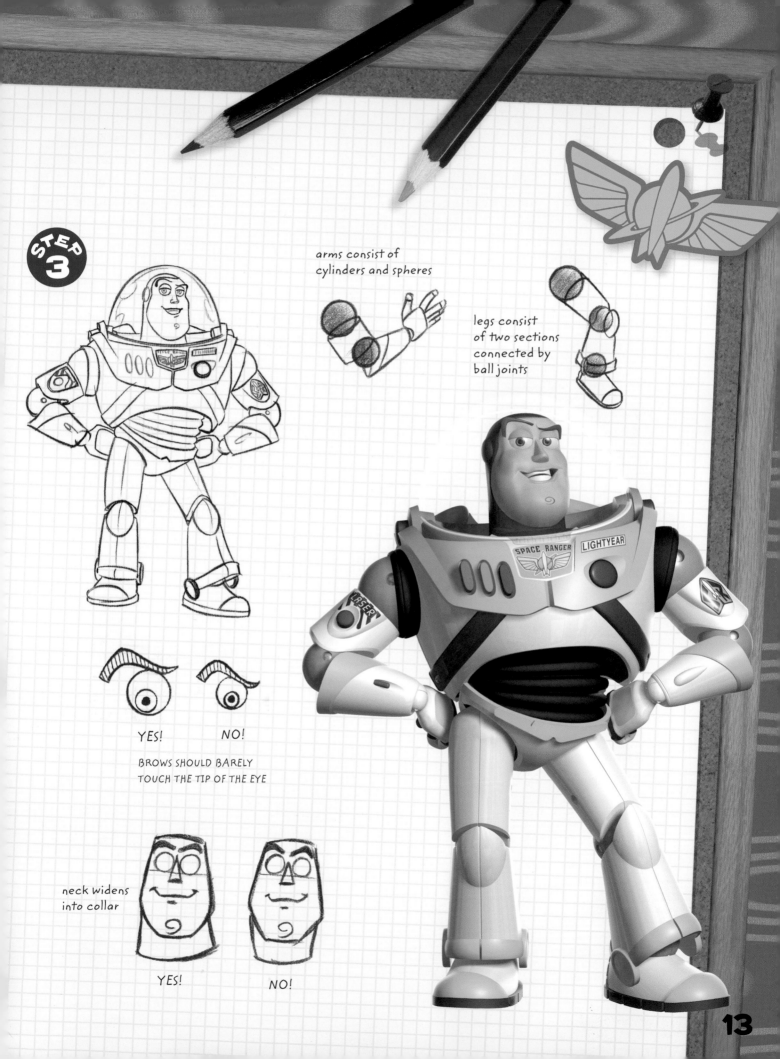

STEP 3

arms consist of
cylinders and spheres

legs consist
of two sections
connected by
ball joints

SPACE RANGER   LIGHTYEAR

YES!   NO!

BROWS SHOULD BARELY
TOUCH THE TIP OF THE EYE

neck widens
into collar

YES!   NO!

13

Jessie

Jessie knows what it means to be a toy. She once belonged to a little girl who loved her as much as Andy loves Woody. But that little girl gave Jessie away and in *Toy Story 2*, the brokenhearted cowgirl decided that being a collectible is better than being with a child who might outgrow you. Woody has to remind Jessie what being a toy is all about. In *Toy Story 3*, Jessie feels the same anxiety about being abandoned by her owner—but this time, it leads the whole gang to danger!

STEP 1

YES! she has a button nose

NO!

3 fringe pieces

stitching wraps around cuff

shirt and gauntlet pattern

don't forget
her ponytail

Woody's hat is
triangular

Jessie's hat is
rounder

STEP 2

her hat usually
sits on the back
of her head

Jessie's body is
flexible like a
rag doll's

STEP 3

BULLSEYE

Bullseye, the sharpest horse in the West, is a trusty, energetic steed that loves Woody more than anything else in the world. This proud pony would do almost anything to keep his favorite sheriff out of harm's way.

STEP 1

YES!
eyes slant
apart slightly

NO!
not too
much

STEP 2

head is
capsule-
shaped

ears roll like felt

bottom of hoof
is shaped like an
upside-down U

legs are loose
and floppy

bottom points
of the tail line up

legs are two
stuffed sections,
almost shaped
like peanuts

STEP
3

REX

This toy dinosaur is one nervous Rex. When he's not worried about being replaced by a bigger dino toy, he's trying to avoid conflict in Andy's room. Rex's growl "almost" scares the other toys.

tail tapers to a point

STEP 1

pear-shaped torso

STEP 2

side of foot

diamond-shaped toenails have a center line

back of foot

keep equal distance between toenails

cone-shaped teeth

Rex's pupils are tiny

basic eye expression

"hmmm."

"what did I step in?"

STEP 3

"the sky is falling!"

legs are thick

MR. POTATO HEAD

Mr. Potato Head can be cranky sometimes, but he's always there when Mrs. Potato Head needs another spud to lean on.

STEP 1

STEP 2

Mr. Potato Head wears gloves

STEP 3

moustache curves down YES!

NO!

large oval-shaped eyes

HAMM

You can always count on Hamm to put in his two cents on any topic. As Andy's piggy bank and Mr. Potato Head's buddy (spuddy?), Hamm says what he thinks...especially when he thinks Woody's headed for trouble.

STEP 1

STEP 2

small ears

eyes can squash and stretch depending on expression

STEP 3

pear-shaped body

three toes

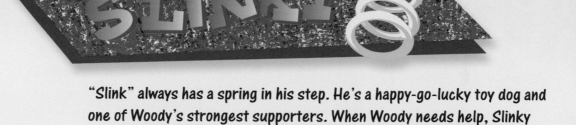

SLINKY

"Slink" always has a spring in his step. He's a happy-go-lucky toy dog and one of Woody's strongest supporters. When Woody needs help, Slinky Dog goes the extra mile—or at least as far as his spring will stretch.

STEP 1

STEP 2

STEP 3

thick, heavy brows

round eyes

head is a ball

Slinky is a pull toy, so he has a wheel on each foot

ALIENS

It's a very small world for the Alien toys at Pizza Planet.
They live to see whom "the Claw" will pluck from their
crane-game world. While trapped inside the crane game,
the Aliens obey the Claw's calling, but once they leave,
they happily switch their loyalty to others—
like Mr. Potato Head, much to his chagrin.

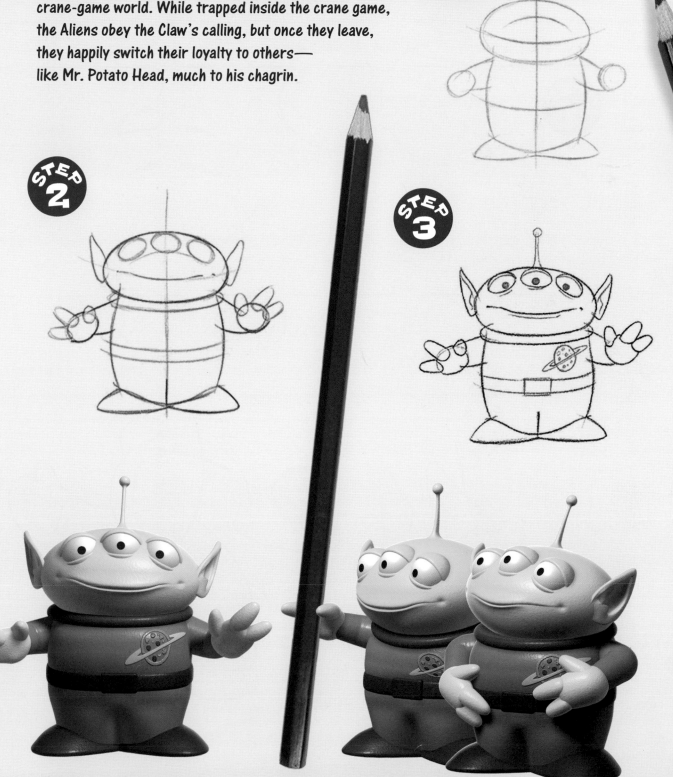

STEP 1

STEP 2

STEP 3

LOTSO

In *Toy Story 3*, Lots-o'-Huggin' Bear—a.k.a Lotso—seems like nothing more than the nicest teddy bear at Sunnyside Daycare. But Lotso's true colors are exposed when he traps Andy's toys in the Caterpillar Room with all of the rambunctious toddlers—and later when he leaves the toys to be incinerated at the garbage dump.

STEP 1

eyebrows are wide and bushy

YES!

NO!

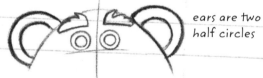
ears are two half circles

nose is an upside-down rounded triangle

teardrop-shaped paws

STEP 2

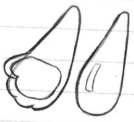

3

STEP 3

eyes are round
and set close
together

His cane is
a wooden
mallet

I'M A HUGGER

BIG BABY

In *Toy Story 3*, Big Baby (along with Lotso and Chuckles) was accidentally left at a rest stop by his first owner, Daisy. Although Big Baby initially does Lotso's dirty work at Sunnyside Daycare, once he realizes how much he misses his mama, he helps the toys escape from Lotso's grasp.

full lips — YES!

— NO!

STEP 1

STEP 2

STEP 3

eyes are oval-shaped; left eye is broken and droops

Big Baby has a curl on his forehead

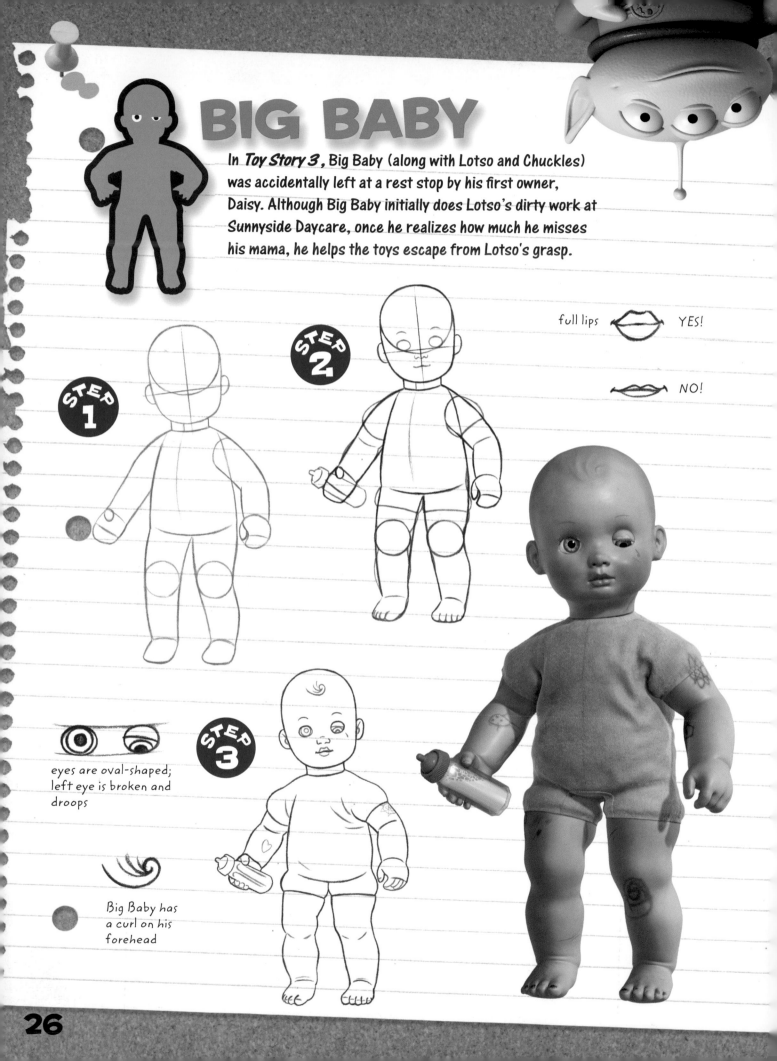

CHUNK

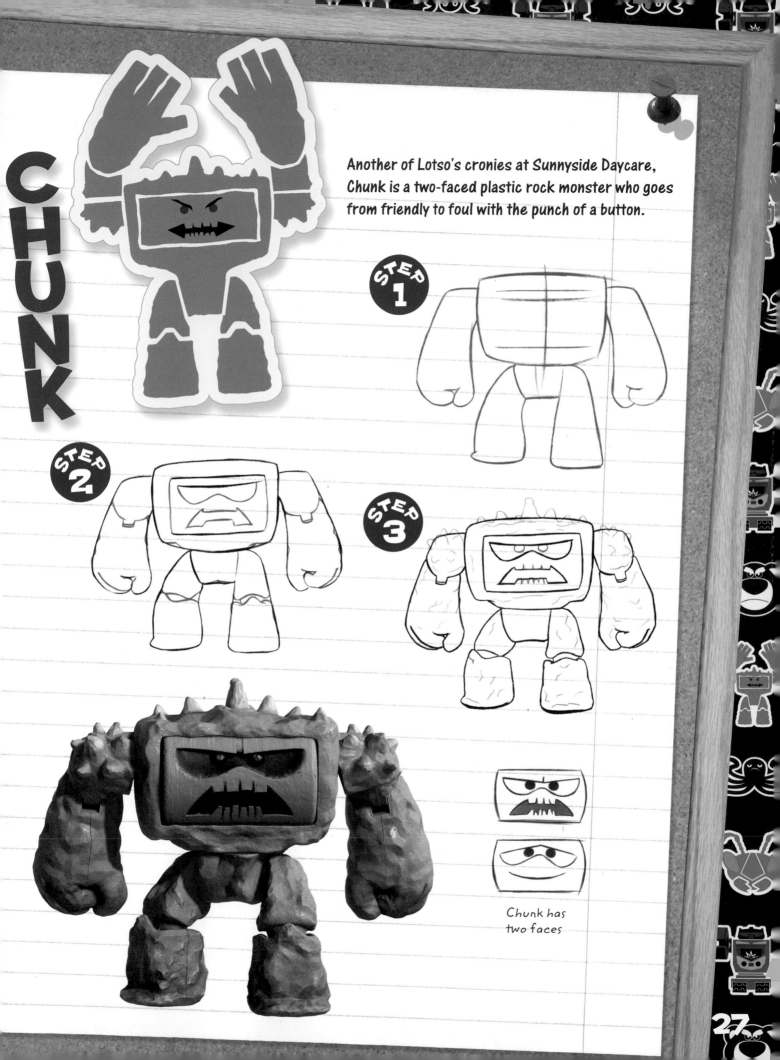

Another of Lotso's cronies at Sunnyside Daycare, Chunk is a two-faced plastic rock monster who goes from friendly to foul with the punch of a button.

STEP **1**

STEP **2**

STEP **3**

Chunk has two faces

MR. PRICKLEPANTS

Mr. Pricklepants is no ordinary hedgehog. This lederhosen-wearing toy is both dramatic and intellectual. He is also very kind to all of the other toys in Bonnie's toy collection.

STEP 1

Mr. Pricklepants is about half Woody's size

STEP 2

body looks like a pear

hat looks like an
upside-down cup
on a saucer

claws
are small
triangles

arms taper

suspenders
have a
buckle

BUTTERCUP

In *Toy Story 3*, Buttercup may look like a cute and cuddly unicorn, but he's really a gruff, no-nonsense member of Bonnie's toy collection.

STEP 1

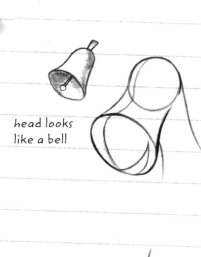

head looks like a bell

STEP 2

body is drawn from simple shapes

tail is short and bushy

STEP 3

horn has
five parts

nostrils
are heart-
shaped

eyes are ovals,
pupils and irises
are round,
eyebrows follow
shape of eye

THE END
Now that you've learned all the tricks to drawing your favorite toys, it's time to have fun! So go ahead—pick up your pencils and draw!